GOSPEL (QUESTIONS) OF ST. BARTHOLOMEW

Anonymous

Table of Contents

GOSPEL (QUESTIONS) OF ST. BARTHOLOMEW

Anonymous

- II
- III
- IV
- V

(the opening 3 verses are given from each of the three texts)

Greek. 1 After the resurrection from the dead of our Lord Jesus Christ, Bartholomew came unto the Lord and questioned him, saying: Lord, reveal unto me the mysteries of the heavens.

2 Jesus answered and said unto him: If I put off the body of the flesh, I shall not be able to tell them unto thee.

3 Om.

Slavonic. 1 Before the resurrection of our Lord Jesus Christ from the dead, the apostles said: Let us question the Lord: Lord, reveal unto us the wonders.

2 And Jesus said unto them: If I put off the body of the flesh, I cannot tell them unto you.

3 But when he was buried and risen again, they all durst not question him, because it was not to look upon him, but the fullness of his Godhead was seen.

4 But Bartholomew,

Latin 2. 1 At that time, before the Lord Jesus Christ suffered, all the disciples were gathered together, questioning him and saying: Lord, show us the mystery in the heavens.

2 But Jesus answered and said unto them: If I put not off the body of flesh I cannot tell you.

3 But after that he had suffered and risen again, all the apostles, looking upon him, durst not question him, because his countenance was not as it had been aforetime, but showed forth the fullness of power.

Greek. 4 Bartholomew therefore drew near unto the Lord and said: I have a word to speak unto thee, Lord.

5 And Jesus said to him: I know what thou art about to say; say then what thou wilt, and I will answer thee.

6 And Bartholomew said: Lord, when thou wentest to be hanged upon the cross, I followed thee afar off and saw thee hung upon the cross, and the angels coming down from heaven and worshipping thee. And when there came darkness, 7 I beheld, and I saw thee that thou wast vanished away from the cross and I heard only a voice in the parts under the earth, and great wailing and gnashing of teeth on a sudden. Tell me, Lord, whither wentest thou from the cross?

8 And Jesus answered and said: Blessed art thou, Bartholomew, my beloved, because thou sawest this mystery, and now will I tell thee all things whatsoever thou askest me. 9 For when I vanished away from the cross, then went I down into Hades that I might bring up Adam and all them that were with him, according to the supplication of Michael the archangel.

GOSPEL (QUESTIONS) OF ST. BARTHOLOMEW

10 Then said Bartholomew: Lord, what was the voice which was heard?

11 Jesus saith unto him: Hades said unto Beliar: As I perceive, a God cometh hither. [Slavonic and latin 2 continue: And the angels cried unto the powers, saying: Remove your gates, ye princes, remove the everlasting doors, for behold the King of glory cometh down.

12 Hades said: Who is the King of glory, that cometh down from heaven unto us?

13 And when I had descended five hundred steps, Hades was troubled, saying: I hear the breathing of the Most High, and I cannot endure it. (latin 2. He cometh with great fragrance and I cannot bear it.) 14 But the devil answered and said: Submit not thyself, O Hades, but be strong: for God himself hath not descended upon the earth. 15 But when I had descended yet five hundred steps, the angels and the powers cried out: Take hold, remove the doors, for behold the King of glory cometh down. And Hades said: O, woe unto me, for I hear the breath of God.]

Greek. 16–17 And Beliar said unto Hades: Look carefully who it is that , for it is Elias, or Enoch, or one of the prophets that this man seemeth to me to be. But Hades answered Death and said: Not yet are six thousand years accomplished. And whence are these, O Beliar; for the sum of the number is in mine hands.

[Slavonic. 16 And the devil said unto Hades: Why affrightest thou me, Hades? it is a prophet, and he hath made himself like unto God: this prophet will we take and bring him hither unto those that think to ascend into heaven. 17 And Hades said: Which of the prophets is it? Show me: Is it Enoch the scribe of righteousness? But God hath not suffered him to come down upon the earth before the end of the six thousand years. Sayest thou that it is Elias, the avenger? But before he cometh not down. What shall I do, whereas the destruction is of God: for surely our end is at hand? For I have the number (of the years) in mine hands.]

Greek. 18 : Be not troubled, make safe thy gates and strengthen thy bars: consider, God cometh not down upon the earth.

19 Hades saith unto him: These be no good words that I hear from thee: my belly is rent, and mine inward parts are pained: it cannot be but that God cometh hither. Alas, whither

shall I flee before the face of the power of the great king? Suffer me to enter into myself (thyself, Latin): for before (of, latin) thee was I formed.

20 Then did I enter in and scourged him and bound him with chains that cannot be loosed, and brought forth thence all the patriarchs and came again unto the cross.

21 Bartholomew saith unto him: [latin 2, I saw thee again, hanging upon the cross, and all the dead arising and worshipping thee, and going up again into their sepulchres.] Tell me, Lord, who was he whom the angels bare up in their hands, even that man that was very great of stature? [Slav., Latin. 2, And what spakest thou unto him that he sighed so sore?]

22 Jesus answered and said unto him: It was Adam the first–formed, for whose sake I came down from heaven upon earth. And I said unto him: I was hung upon the cross for thee and for thy children's sake. And he, when he heard it, groaned and said: So was thy good pleasure, O Lord.

23 Again Bartholomew said: Lord, I saw the angels ascending before Adam and singing praises.

24 But one of the angels which was very great, above the rest, would not ascend up with them: and there was in his hand a sword of fire, and he was looking steadfastly upon thee only.

[Slav. 25 And all the angels besought him that he would go up with them, but he would not. But when thou didst command him to go up, I beheld a flame of fire issuing out of his hands and going even unto the city of Jerusalem. 26 And Jesus said unto him: Blessed art thou, Bartholomew my beloved because thou sawest these mysteries. This was one of the angels of vengeance which stand before my Father's throne: and this angel sent he unto me. 27 And for this cause he would not ascend up, because he desired to destroy all the powers of the world. But when I commanded him to ascend up, there went a flame out of his hand and rent asunder the veil of the temple, and parted it in two pieces for a witness unto the children of Israel for my passion because they crucified me. (Lat. 1. But the flame which thou sawest issuing out of his hands smote the house of the synagogue of the Jews, for a testimony of me wherein they crucified me.)].

Greek. 28 And when he had thus spoken, he said unto the apostles: Tarry for me in this place, for today a sacrifice is offered in paradise. 29 And Bartholomew answered and said unto Jesus: Lord, what is the sacrifice which is offered in paradise? And Jesus said: There be souls of the righteous which to-day have departed out of the body and go unto paradise, and unless I be present they cannot enter into paradise.

30 And Bartholomew said: Lord, how many souls depart out of the world daily? Jesus saith unto him: Thirty thousand.

31 Bartholomew saith unto him: Lord, when thou wast with us teaching the word, didst thou receive the sacrifices in paradise? Jesus answered and said unto him: Verily I say unto thee, my beloved, that I both taught the word with you and continually sat with my Father, and received the sacrifices in paradise everyday. 32 Bartholomew answered and said unto him: Lord, if thirty thousand souls depart out of the world every day, how many souls out of them are found righteous? Jesus saith unto him: Hardly fifty [three] my beloved. 33 Again Bartholomew saith: And how do three only enter into paradise? Jesus saith unto him: The [fifty] three enter into paradise or are laid up in Abraham's bosom: but the others go into the place of the resurrection, for the three are not like unto the fifty.

34 Bartholomew saith unto him: Lord, how many souls above the number are born into the world daily? Jesus saith unto him: One soul only is born above the number of them that depart.[30, Latin 1. Bartholomew said: How many are the souls which depart out of the body every day? Jesus said: Verily I say unto thee, twelve (thousand) eight hundred, four score and three souls depart out of the body every day.]

35 And when he had said this he gave them the peace, and vanished away from them.

II

1 ow the apostles were in the place [Cherubim, Cheltoura, Chritir] with Mary. 2 And Bartholomew came and said unto Peter and Andrew and John: Let us ask her that is highly favoured how she conceived the incomprehensible, or how she bare him that cannot be carried, or how she brought forth so much greatness. But they doubted to ask her. 3 Bartholomew therefore said unto Peter: Thou that art the chief, and my teacher, draw near and ask her. But Peter said to John: Thou art a virgin and undefiled (and beloved) and thou must ask her.

4 And as they all doubted and disputed, Bartholomew came near unto her with a cheerful countenance and said to her: Thou that art highly favoured, the tabernacle of the Most High, unblemished we, even all the apostles, ask thee (or All the apostles have sent me to ask thee) to tell us how thou didst conceive the incomprehensible, or how thou didst bear him that cannot be carried, or how thou didst bring forth so much greatness.

5 But Mary said unto them: Ask me not (or Do ye indeed ask me) concerning this mystery. If I should begin to tell you, fire will issue forth out of my mouth and consume all the world.

6 But they continued yet the more to ask her. And she, for she could not refuse to hear the apostles, said: Let us stand up in prayer. 7 And the apostles stood behind Mary: but she said unto Peter: Peter, thou chief, thou great pillar, standest thou behind us? Said not our Lord: the head of the man is Christ ? now therefore stand ye before me and pray. 8 But they said unto her: In thee did the Lord set his tabernacle, and it was his good pleasure that thou shouldest contain him, and thou oughtest to be the leader in the prayer (al. to go with us to). 9 But she said unto them: Ye are shining stars, and as the prophet said, 'I did lift up mine eyes unto the hills, from whence shall come mine help'; ye, therefore, are the hills, and it behoveth you to pray.

10 The apostles say unto her: Thou oughtest to pray, thou art the mother of the heavenly king. 11 Mary saith unto them: In your likeness did God form the sparrows, and sent them forth into the four corners of the world. 12 But they say unto her: He that is scarce contained by the seven heavens was pleased to be contained in thee.

13 Then Mary stood up before them and spread out her hands toward the heaven and began to speak thus: Elphue Zarethra Charboum Nemioth Melitho Thraboutha Mephnounos Chemiath Aroura Maridon Elison Marmiadon Seption Hesaboutha Ennouna Saktinos Athoor Belelam Opheoth Abo Chrasar (this is the reading of one Greek copy: the others and the Slavonic have many differences as in all such cases: but as the original words—assuming them to have once had a meaning—are hopelessly corrupted, the matter is not of importancc), which is in the Greek tongue(Hebrew, Slav.): O God the exceeding great and all—wise and king of the worlds (ages), that art not to be described, the ineffable, that didst establish the greatness of the heavens and all things by a word, that out of darkness (or the unknown) didst constitute and fasten together the poles of heaven in harmony, didst bring into shape the matter that was in confusion, didst bring into order the things that were without order, didst part the misty darkness from the light, didst establish in one place the foundations of the waters, thou that makest the beings of the air to tremble, and art the fear of them that are on (or under) the earth, that didst settle the earth and not suffer it to perish, and filledst it, which is the nourisher of all things, with showers of blessing: (Son of) the Father, thou whom the seven heavens hardly contained, but who wast well—pleased to be contained without pain in me, thou that art thyself the full word of the Father in whom all things came to be: give glory to thine exceeding great name, and bid me to speak before thy holy apostles .

14 And when she had ended the prayer she began to say unto them: Let us sit down upon the ground; and come thou, Peter the chief, and sit on my right hand and put thy left hand beneath mine armpit; and thou, Andrew, do so on my left hand; and thou, John, the virgin, hold together my bosom; and thou, Bartholomew, set thy knees against my back and hold my shoulders, lest when I begin to speak my bones be loosed one from another.

15 And when they had so done she began to say: When I abode in the temple of God and received my food from an angel, on a certain day there appeared unto me one in the likeness of an angel, but his face was incomprehensible, and he had not in his hand bread or a cup, as did the angel which came to me aforetime.

16 And straightway the robe (veil) of the temple was rent and there was a very great earthquake, and I fell upon the earth, for I was not able to endure the sight of him. 17 But he put his hand beneath me and raised me up, and I looked up into heaven and there came a cloud of dew and sprinkled me from the head to the feet, and he wiped me with his robe. 18 And said unto me: Hail, thou that art highly favoured, the chosen vessel, grace

inexhaustible. And he smote his garment upon the right hand and there came a very great loaf, and he set it upon the altar of the temple and did eat of it first himself, and gave unto me also. 19 And again he smote his garment upon the left hand and there came a very great cup full of wine: and he set it upon the altar of the temple and did drink of it first himself, and gave also unto me. And I beheld and saw the bread and the cup whole as they were.

20 And he said unto me: Yet three years, and I will send my word unto thee and then shalt conceive my (or a) son, and through him shall the whole creation be saved. Peace be unto thee, my beloved, and my peace shall be with thee continually.

21 And when he had so said he vanished away from mine eyes, and the temple was restored as it had been before.

22 And as she was saying this, fire issued out of her mouth; and the world was at the point to come to an end: but Jesus appeared quickly (lat. 2, and laid his hand upon her mouth) and said unto Mary: Utter not this mystery, or this day my whole creation will come to an end (Lat. 2, and the flame from her mouth ceased). And the apostles were taken with fear lest haply the Lord should be wroth with them.

III

1 And he departed with them unto the mount Mauria (Lat. 2, Mambre), and sat in the midst of them. 2 But they doubted to question him, being afraid. 3 And Jesus answered and said unto them: Ask me what ye will that I should teach you, and I will show it you. For yet seven days, and I ascend unto my Father, and I shall no more be seen of you in this likeness. 4 But they, yet doubting, said unto him: Lord, show us the deep (abyss) according unto thy promise. 5 And Jesus said unto them: It is not good (Lat. 2, is good) for you to see the deep: notwithstanding, if ye desire it, according to my promise, come, follow me and behold. 6 And he led them away into a place that is called Cherubim (Cherukt Slav., Chairoudee Gr., Lat. 2 omits), that is the place of truth. 7 And he beckoned unto the angels of the West and the earth was rolled up like a volume of a book and the deep was revealed unto them. 8 And when the apostles saw it they fell on their faces upon the earth. 9 But Jesus raised them up, saying: Said I not unto you, 'It is not good for you to see the deep'. And again he beckoned unto the angels, and the deep was covered up.

IV

1 And he took them and brought them again unto the Mount of olives.

2 And Peter said unto Mary: Thou that art highly favoured, entreat the Lord that he would reveal unto us the things that are in the heavens.

3 And Mary said unto Peter: O stone hewn out of the rock, did not the Lord build his church upon thee? Go thou therefore first and ask him.

4 Peter saith again: O tabernacle that art spread abroad . 5 Mary saith: Thou art the image of Adam: was not he first formed and then Eve? Look upon the sun, that according to the likeness of Adam it is bright. and upon the moon, that because of the transgression of Eve it is full of clay. For God did place Adam in the east and Eve in the west, and appointed the lights that the sun should shine on the earth unto Adam in the east in his fiery chariots, and the moon in the west should give light unto Eve with a countenance like milk. And she defiled the commandment of the Lord. Therefore was the moon stained with clay (Lat. 2, is cloudy) and her light is not bright. Thou therefore, since thou art the likeness of Adam, oughtest to ask him: but in me was he contained that I might recover the strength of the female.

6 Now when they came up to the top of the mount, and the Master was withdrawn from them a little space, Peter saith unto Mary: Thou art she that hast brought to nought the transgression of Eve, changing it from shame into joy; it is lawful, therefore, for thee to ask.

7 When Jesus appeared again, Bartholomew saith unto him: Lord, show us the adversary of men that we may behold him, of what fashion he is, and what is his work, and whence he cometh forth, and what power he hath that he spared not even thee, but caused thee to be hanged upon the tree. 8 But Jesus looked upon him and said: Thou bold heart! thou askest for that which thou art not able to look upon. 9 But Bartholomew was troubled and fell at Jesus' feet and began to speak thus: O lamp that cannot be quenched, Lord Jesu Christ, maker of the eternal light that hast given unto them that love thee the grace that beautifieth all, and hast given us the eternal light by thy coming into the world, that hast accomplished the work of the Father, hast turned the shame–facedness of Adam into

mirth, hast done away the sorrow of Eve with a cheerful countenance by thy birth from a virgin: remember not evil against me but grant me the word of mine asking. (Lat. 2, who didst come down into the world, who hast confirmed the eternal word of the Father, who hast called the sadness of joy, who hast made the shame of Eve glad, and restored her by vouchsafing to be contained in the womb.)

10 And as he thus spake, Jesus raised him up and said unto him: Bartholomew, wilt thou see the adversary of men? I tell thee that when thou beholdest him, not thou only but the rest of the apostles and Mary will fall on your faces and become as dead corpses.

11 But they all said unto him: Lord, let us behold him.

12 And he led them down from the Mount of Olives and looked wrathfully upon the angels that keep hell (Tartarus), and beckoned unto Michael to sound the trumpet in the height of the heavens. And Michael sounded, and the earth shook, and Beliar came up, being held by 660 (560 Gr., 6,064 Lat. 1, 6,060 Lat. 2) angels and bound with fiery chains. 12 And the length of him was 1,600 cubits and his breadth 40 (Lat. 1, 300, Slav. 17) cubits (Lat. 2, his length 1,900 cubits, his breadth 700, one wing of him 80), and his face was like a lightning of fire and his eyes full of darkness (like sparks, Slav.). And out of his nostrils came a stinking smoke; and his mouth was as the gulf of a precipice, and the one of his wings was four–score cubits. 14 And straightway when the apostles saw him, they fell to the earth on their faces and became as dead. 15 But Jesus came near and raised the apostles and gave them a spirit of power, and he saith unto Bartholomew: Come near, Bartholomew, and trample with thy feet on his neck, and he will tell thee his work, what it is, and how he deceiveth men. 16 And Jesus stood afar off with the rest of the apostles. 17 And Barthololmew feared, and raised his voice and said: Blessed be the name of thine immortal kingdom from henceforth even for ever. And when he had spoken, Jesus permitted him, saying: Go and tread upon the neck of Beliar: and Bartholomew ran quickly upon him and trode upon his neck: and Beliar trembled. (For this verse the Vienna MS. has: And Bartholomew raised his voice and said thus: O womb more spacious than a city, wider than the spreading of the heavens, that contained him whom the seven heavens contain not, but thou without pain didst contain sanctified in thy bosom, evidently out of place. Latin 1 has only: Then did Antichrist tremble and was filled with fury.)

18 And Bartholomew was afraid, and fled, and said unto Jesus: Lord, give me an hem of thy garments (Lat. 2, the kerchief (?) from thy shoulders) that I may have courage to draw near unto him. 19 But Jesus said unto him: Thou canst not take an hem of my garments, for these are not my garments which I wore before I was crucified. 20 And Bartholomew said: Lord, I fear Iest, like as he spared not thine angels, he swallow me up also. 21 Jesus saith unto him: Were not all things made by my word, and by the will of my Father the spirits were made subject unto Solomon? thou, therefore, being commanded by my word, go in my name and ask him what thou wilt. (lat. 2 omits 20.) 22 [And Bartholomew made the sign of the cross and prayed unto Jesus and went behind him. And Jesus said to him: Draw near. And as Bartholomew drew near, fire was kindled on every side, so that his garments appeared fiery. Jesus saith to Bartholomew: As I said unto thee, tread upon his neck and ask him what is his power.] And Bartholomew went and trode upon his neck, and pressed down his face into the earth as far as his ears. 23 And Bartholomew saith unto him: Tell me who thou art and what is thy name. And he said to him: Lighten me a little, and I will tell thee who I am and how I came hither, and what my work is and what my power is. 24 And he lightened him and saith to him: Say all that thou hast done and all that thou doest. 25 And Beliar answered and said: If thou wilt know my name, at the first I was called Satanael, which is interpreted a messenger of God, but when I rejected the image of God my name was called Satanas, that is, an angel that keepeth hell (Tartarus). 26 And again Bartholomew saith unto him: Reveal unto me all things and hide nothing from me. 27 And he said unto him: I swear unto thee by the power of the glory of God that even if I would hide aught I cannot, for he is near that would convict me. For if I were able I would have destroyed you like one of them that were before you. 28 For, indeed, I was formed (al. called) the first angel: for when God made the heavens, he took a handful of fire and formed me first, Michael second [Vienna MS. here has these sentences: for he had his Son before the heavens and the earth and we were formed (for when he took thought to create all things, his Son spake a word), so that we also were created by the will of the Son and the consent of the Father. He formed, I say, first me, next Michael the chief captain of the hosts that are above], Gabriel third, Uriel fourth, Raphael fifth, Nathanael sixth, and other angels of whom I cannot tell the names. [Jerusalem MS., Michael, Gabriel, Raphael, Uriel, Xathanael, and other 6,000 angels. Lat. I, Michael the honour of power, third Raphael, fourth Gabriel, and other seven. Lat. 2, Raphael third, Gabriel fourth, Uriel fifth, Zathael sixth, and other six.] For they are the rod–bearers (lictors) of God, and they smite me with their rods and pursue me seven times in the night and seven times in the day, and leave me not at all and break in pieces all my power. These are the (twelve, lat. 2) angels of vengeance which stand before the

throne of God: these are the angels that were first formed. 30 And after them were formed all the angels. In the first heaven are an hundred myriads, and in the second an hundred myriads, and in the third an hundred myriads, and in the fourth an hundred myriads, and in the fifth an hundred myriads, and in the sixth an hundred myriads, and in the seventh (an hundred myriads, and outside the seven heavens, Jerusalem MS.) is the first firmament (flat surface) wherein are the powers which work upon men. 31 For there are four other angels set over the winds. The first angel is over the north, and he is called Chairoum (. . . broil, Jerusalem MS.; lat. 2, angel of the north, Mauch), and hath in his hand a rod of fire, and restraineth the super–fluity of moisture that the earth be not overmuch wet. 32 And the angel that is over the north is called Oertha (Lat. 2, Alfatha): he hath a torch of fire and putteth it to his sides, and they warm the great coldness of him that he freeze not the world. 33 And the angel that is over the south is called Kerkoutha (Lat. 2, Cedar) and they break his fierceness that he shake not the earth. 34 And the angel that is over the south–west is called Naoutha, and he hath a rod of snow in his hand and putteth it into his mouth, and quencheth the fire that cometh out of his mouth. And if the angel quenched it not at his mouth it would set all the world on fire. 35 And there is another angel over the sea which maketh it rough with the waves thereof. 36 But the rest I will not tell thee, for he that standeth by suffereth me not.

37 Bartholomew saith unto him: Flow chastisest thou the souls of men? 38 Beliar saith unto him: Wilt thou that I declare unto thee the punishment of the hypocrites, of the back–biters, of the jesters, of the idolaters, and the covetous, and the adulterers, and the wizards, and the diviners, and of them that believe in us, and of all whom I look upon (deceive?)? (38 Lat. 2: When I will show any illusion by them. But they that do these things, and they that consent unto them or follow them, do perish with me. 39 Bartholomew said unto him: Declare quickly how thou persuadest men not to follow God and thine evil arts, that are slippery and dark, that they should leave the straight and shining paths of the Lord.) 39 Bartholomew saith unto him: I will that thou declare it in few words. 40 And he smote his teeth together, gnashing them, and there came up out of the bottomless pit a wheel having a sword flashing with fire, and in the sword were pipes. 41 And I (he) asked him, saying: What is this sword? 42 And he said: This sword is the sword of the gluttonous: for into this pipe are sent they that through their gluttony devise all manner of sin; into the second pipe are sent the backbiters which backbite their neighbour secretly; into the third pipe are sent the hypocrites and the rest whom I overthrow by my contrivance. (Lat. 2:40 And Antichrist said: I will tell thee. And a wheel came up out of the abyss, having seven fiery knives. The first knife hath twelve pipes

13

(canales).. . . 42 Antichrist answered: The pipe of fire in the first knife, in it are put the casters of lots and diviners and enchanters, and they that believe in them or have sought them, because in the iniquity of their heart they have invented false divinations. In the second pipe of fire are first the blasphemers ... suicides ... idolaters.... In the rest are first perjurers . . . (long enumeration).) 43 And Bartholomew said: Dost thou then do these things by thyself alone? 44 And Satan said: If I were able to go forth by myself, I would have destroyed the whole world in three days: but neither I nor any of the six hundred go forth. For we have other swift ministers whom we command, and we furnish them with an hook of many points and send them forth to hunt, and they catch for us souls of men, enticing them with sweetness of divers baits, that is by drunkenness and laughter, by backbiting, hypocrisy, pleasures, fornication, and the rest of the trifles that come out of their treasures. (Lat. 2 amplifies enormously.)

45 And I will tell thee also the rest of the names of the angels. The angel of the hail is called Mermeoth, and he holdeth the hail upon his head, and my ministers do adjure him and send him whither they will. And other angels are there over the snow, and other over the thunder, and other over the lightning, and when any spirit of us would go forth either by land or by sea, these angels send forth fiery stones and set our limbs on fire. (Lat. 2 enumerates all the transgressions of Israel and all possible sins in two whole pages.)

46 Bartholomew saith: Be still (be muzzled) thou dragon of the pit. 47 And Beliar said: Many things will I tell thee of the angels. They that run together throughout the heavenly places and the earthly are these: Mermeoth, Onomatath, Douth, Melioth, Charouth, Graphathas, Oethra, Nephonos, Chalkatoura. With them do fly (are administered?) the things that are in heaven and on earth and under the earth.

48 Bartholomew saith unto him: Be still (be muzzled) and be faint, that I may entreat my Lord. 49 And Bartholomew fell upon his face and cast earth upon his head and began to say: O Lord Jesu Christ, the great and glorious name. All the choirs of the angels praise thee, O Master, and I that am unworthy with my lips . . . do praise thee, O Master. Hearken unto me thy servant, and as thou didst choose me from the receipt of custom and didst not suffer me to have my conversation unto the end in my former deeds, O Lord Jesu Christ, hearken unto me and have mercy upon the sinners. 50 And when he had so said, the Lord saith unto him: Rise up, suffer him that groaneth to arise: I will declare the rest unto thee. 51 And Bartholomew raised up Satan and said unto him: Go unto thy place, with thine angels, but the Lord hath mercy upon all his world. (50, 51, again

enormously amplified in lat. 2. Satan complains that he has been tricked into telling his secrets before the time. The interpolation is to some extent dated by this sentence: ' Simon Magus and Zaroes and Arfaxir and Jannes and Mambres are my brothers.' Zaroes and Arfaxatare wizards who figure in the Latin Acts of Matthew and of Simon and Jude (see below). 49 follows 51 in this text.)

52 But the devil said: Suffer me, and I will tell thee how I was cast down into this place and how the Lord did make man. 53 I was going to and fro in the world, and God said unto Michael: Bring me a clod from the four corners of the earth, and water out of the four rivers of paradise. And when Michael brought them God formed Adam in the regions of the east, and shaped the clod which was shapeless, and stretched sinews and veins upon it and established it with Joints; and he worshipped him, himself for his own sake first, because he was the image of God, therefore he worshipped him. 54 And when I came from the ends of the earth Michael said: Worship thou the image of God, which he hath made according to his likeness. But I said: I am fire of fire, I was the first angel formed, and shall worship clay and matter? 55 And Michael saith to me: Worship, lest God be wroth with thee. But I said to him: God will not be wroth with me; but I will set my throne over against his throne, and I will be as he is. Then was God wroth with me and cast me down, having commanded the windows of heaven to be opened. 56 And when I was cast down, he asked also the six hundred that were under me, if they would worship: but they said: Like as we have seen the first angel do, neither will we worship him that is less than ourselves. Then were the six hundred also cast down by him with me. 57 And when we were cast down upon the earth we were senseless for forty years, and when the sun shone forth seven times brighter than fire, suddenly I awaked; and I looked about and saw the six hundred that were under me senseless. 58 And I awaked my son Salpsan and took him to counsel how I might deceive the man on whose account I was cast out of the heavens. 59 And thus did I contrive it. I took a vial in mine hand and scraped the sweat from off my breast and the hair of mine armpits, and washed myself (Lat. 2, I took fig leaves in my hands and wiped the sweat from my bosom and below mine arms and cast it down beside the streams of waters. 69 is greatly prolonged in this text) in the springs of the waters whence the four rivers flow out, and Eve drank of it and desire came upon her: for if she had not drunk of that water I should not have been able to deceive her. 60 Then Bartholomew commanded him to go into hell.

61 And Bartholomew came and fell at Jesus' feet and began with tears to say thus: Abba, Father, that art past finding out by us, Word of the Father, whom the seven heavens

hardly contained, but who wast pleased to be contained easily and without pain within the body of the Virgin: whom the Virgin knew not that she bare: thou by thy thought hast ordained all things to be: thou givest us that which we need before thou art entreated. 62 Thou that didst wear a crown of thorns that thou mightest prepare for us that repent the precious crown from heaven; that didst hang upon the tree, that (a clause gone): (lat. 2, that thou mightest turn from us the tree of lust and concupiscence (etc., etc.). The verse is prolonged for over 40 lines) (that didst drink wine mingled with gall) that thou mightest give us to drink of the wine of compunction, and wast pierced n the side with a spear that thou mightest fill us with thy body and thy blood: 63 Thou that gavest names unto the four rivers: to the first Phison, because of the faith (pistis) which thou didst appear in the world to preach; to the second Geon, for that man was made of earth (ge); to the third Tigris, because by thee was revealed unto us the consubstantial Trinity in the heavens (to make anything of this we must read Trigis); to the fourth Euphrates, because by thy presence in the world thou madest every soul to rejoice (euphranai) through the word of immortality. 64 My God, and Father, the greatest, my King: save, Lord, the sinners. 65 When he had thus prayed Jesus said unto him: Bartholomew, my Father did name me Christ, that I might come down upon earth and anoint every man that cometh unto me with the oil of life: and he did call me Jesus that I might heal every sin of them that know not . . . and give unto men (several corrupt words: the Latin has) the truth of God.

66 And again Bartholomew saith unto him: Lord, is it lawful for me to reveal these mysteries unto every man? Jesus saith unto him: Bartholomew, my beloved, as many as are faithful and are able to keep them unto themselves, to them mayest thou entrust these things. For some there are that be worthy of them, but there are also other some unto whom it is not fit to entrust them: for they are vain (swaggerers), drunkards, proud, unmerciful, partakers in idolatry, authors of fornication, slanderers, teachers of foolishness, and doing all works that are of the devil, and therefore are they not worthy that these should be entrusted to them. 68 And also they are secret, because of those that cannot contain them; for as many as can contain them shall have a part in them. Herein (Hitherto?) therefore, my beloved, have I spoken unto thee, for blessed art thou and all thy kindred which of their choice have this word entrusted unto them; for all they that can contain it shall receive whatsoever they will in the of my judgement.

69 Then I, Bartholomew, which wrote these things in mine heart, took hold on the hand of the lord the lover of men and began to rejoice and to speak thus:

GOSPEL (QUESTIONS) OF ST. BARTHOLOMEW

Glory be to thee, O Lord Jesus Christ, that givest unto all thy grace which all we have perceived. Alleluia.

Glory be to thee, O Lord, the life of sinners.

Glory be to thee, O Lord, death is put to shame.

Glory be to thee, O Lord, the treasure of righteousness.

For unto God do we sing.

70 And as Bartholomew thus spake again, Jesus put off his mantle and took a kerchief from the neck of Bartholomew and began to rejoice and say (70 lat. 2, Then Jesus took a kerchief (?) I and said: I am good: mild and gracious and merciful, strong and righteous, wonderful and holy): I am good. Alleluia. I am meek and gentle. Alleluia. Glory be to thee, O Lord: for I give gifts unto all them that desire me. Alleluia.

Glory be to thee, O Lord, world without end. Amen. Alleluia.

71 And when he had ceased, the apostles kissed him, and he gave them the peace of love.

V

1 Bartholomew saith unto him: Declare unto us, Lord what sin is heavier than all sins? 2 Jesus saith unto him: Verily I say unto thee that hypocrisy and backbiting is heavier than all sins: for because of them, the prophet said in the psalm, that 'the ungodly shall not rise in the judgement, neither sinners in the council of the righteous', neither the ungodly in the judgement of my Father. Verily, verily, I say unto you, that every sin shall be forgiven unto every man, but the sin against the Holy Ghost shall not be forgiven. 3 And Bartholomew saith unto him: What is the sin against the Holy Ghost? 4 Jesus saith unto him: Whosoever shall decree against any man that hath served my holy Father hath blasphemed against the Holy Ghost: For every man that serveth God worshipfully is worthy of the Holy Ghost, and he that speaketh anything evil against him shall not be forgiven.

5 Woe unto him that sweareth by the head of God, yea woe (?) to him that sweareth falsely by him truly. For there are twelve heads of God the most high: for he is the truth, and in him is no lie, neither forswearing. 6 Ye, therefore, go ye and preach unto all the world the word of truth, and thou, Bartholomew, preach this word unto every one that desireth it; and as many as believe thereon shall have eternal life.

7 Bartholomew saith: O Lord, and if any sin with sin of the body, what is their reward? 8 And Jesus said: It is good if he that is baptized present his baptism blameless: but the pleasure of the flesh will become a lover. For a single marriage belongeth to sobriety: for verily I say unto thee, he that sinneth after the third marriage (wife) is unworthy of God. (8 Lat. 2 is to this effect: . . . But if the lust of the flesh come upon him, he ought to be the husband of one wife. The married, if they are good and pay tithes, will receive a hundredfold. A second marriage is lawful, on condition of the diligent performance of good works, and due payment of tithes: but a third marriage is reprobated: and virginity is best.) 9 But ye, preach ye unto every man that they keep themselves from such things: for I depart not from you and I do supply you with the Holy Ghost. (lat. 2, At the end of 9, Jesus ascends in the clouds, and two angels appear and say: 'Ye men of Galilee', and the rest) 10 And Bartholomew worshipped him with the apostles, and glorified God earnestly, saying: Glory be to thee, Holy Father, Sun unquenchable, incomprehensible, full of light. Unto thee be glory, unto thee honour and adoration, world without end. Amen. (Lat. 2, End of the questioning of the most blessed Bartholomew and (or) the

other apostles with the Lord Jesus Christ.)

THE BOOK OF THE RESURRECTION OF CHRIST BY BARTHOLOMEW THE APOSTLE

This exists in Coptic only. There are several recensions of it: the most complete is in a manuscript recently acquired by the British Museum (Or. 6804), and translated first by W. E. Crum (Rustafjaell's light of Egypt, 1910) and then edited and translated by Sir E. A. Wallis Budge (Coptic Apocrypha in the dialect of Upper Egypt, 1913). Other fragments are in the publications of Lacau and Revillout. No full translation, but only an analysis, will be offered here. Five leaves are wanting at the beginning of the British Museum MS. The contents of these can be partly filled up from Lacau and Revillout. But in the first place a passage (p. 193, Budge) may be quoted which shows something of the setting of the book: 'Do not let this book come into the hand of any man who is an unbeliever and a heretic. Behold this is the seventh time that I have commanded thee, O my son Thaddaeus, concerning these mysteries. Reveal not thou them to any impure man, but keep them safely. ' We see that the book was addressed by Bartholomew to his son Thaddaeus, and this would no doubt have been the subject of some of the opening lines of the text.

Next we may place the two fragments, one about the child of Joseph of Arimathaea, the other about the cock raised to life, which have been already described as nos. 7 and 8 of the Coptic narratives of the Passion (pp. 149, 150). The order is uncertain. Then we have a piece which in Revillout is no. 12 (p. 165), in Lacauno. 3 (p. 34). Lacau gives it partly in two recensions.

Christ is on the cross, but his side has been pierced, and he is dead.

A man in the crowd named Ananias, of Bethlehem, rushes to the cross and embraces and salutes the body breast to breast, hand to hand, and denounces the Jews. A voice comes from the body of Jesus and blesses Ananias, promising him incorruption and the name of ' the firstfruits of the immortal fruit '. The priests decide to stone Ananias: he utters words of exultation. The stoning produces no effect. They cast him into a furnace where he remains till Jesus has risen. At last they pierce him with a spear.

The Saviour takes his soul to heaven, and blesses him.

GOSPEL (QUESTIONS) OF ST. BARTHOLOMEW

There can be but little matter lost between this and the opening of the British Museum MS., in the first lines of which the taking of Ananias' soul to heaven is mentioned.

We now take up the British Museum MS. as our basis. Certain passages of it are preserved in Paris fragments which partly overlap each other, and so three different texts exist for some parts: but it will not be important for our purpose to note many of the variations.

Joseph of Arimathaea buried the body of Jesus. Death came into Amente (the underworld), asking who the new arrival was, for he detected a disturbance.

He came to the tomb of Jesus with his six sons in the form of serpents. Jesus lay there (it was the second day, i. e. the Saturday) with his face and head covered with napkins.

Death addressed his son the Pestilence, and described the commotion which had taken place in his domain. Then he spoke to the body of Jesus and asked, 'Who art thou?' Jesus removed the napkin that was on his face and looked in the face of Death and laughed at him. Death and his sons fled. Then they approached again, and the same thing happened. He addressed Jesus again at some length, suspecting, but not certain, who he was.

Then Jesus rose and mounted into the chariot of the Cherubim. He wrought havoc in Hell, breaking the doors, binding the demons Beliar and Melkir (cf. Melkira in the Ascension of Isaiah), and delivered Adam and the holy souls.

Then he turned to Judas Iscariot and uttered a long rebuke, and described the sufferings which he must endure. Thirty names of sins are given, which are the snakes which were sent to devour him.

Jesus rose from the dead, and Abbaton (Death) and Pestilence came back to Amente to protect it, but they found it wholly desolate, only three souls were left in it (those of Herod, Cain, and Judas, says the Paris MS.).

Meanwhile the angels were singing the hymn which the Seraphim sing at dawn on the Lord's day over his body and his blood.

GOSPEL (QUESTIONS) OF ST. BARTHOLOMEW

Early in the morning of the Lord's day the women went to the tomb. They were Mary Magdalene, Mary the mother of James whom Jesus delivered out of the hand of Satan, Salome who tempted him, Mary who ministered to him and Martha her sister, Joanna (al. Susanna) the wife of Chuza who had renounced the marriage bed, Berenice who was healed of an issue of blood in Capernaum, Lia (Leah) the widow whose son he raised at Nain, and the woman to whom he said, 'Thy sins which are many are forgiven thee'.

These were all in the garden of Philogenes, whose son Simeon Jesus healed when he came down from the Mount of Olives with the apostles (probably the lunatic boy at the Mount of Transfiguration).

Mary said to Philogenes: If thou art indeed he, I know thee. Philogenes said: Thou art Mary the mother of Thalkamarimath, which means joy, blessing, and gladness. Mary said: If thou have borne him away, tell me where thou hast laid him and I will take him away: fear not. Philogenes told how the Jews sought a safe tomb for Jesus that the body might not be stolen, and he offered to place it in a tomb in his own garden and watch over it: and they sealed it and departed. At midnight he rose and went out and found all the orders of angels: Cherubim Seraphim, Powers, and Virgins. Heaven opened, and the Father raised Jesus. Peter, too, was there and supported Philogenes, or he would have died.

The Saviour then appeared to them on the chariot of the Father and said to Mary: Mari Khar Mariath (Mary the mother of the Son of God). Mary answered: Rabbouni Kathiathari Mioth (The Son of God the Almighty, my Lord, and my Son.). A long address to Mary from Jesus follows, in the course of which he bids her tell his brethren, 'I ascend unto my Father and your Father', Mary says: If indeed I am not permitted to touch thee, at least bless my body in which thou didst deign to dwell.

Believe me, my brethren the holy apostles, I, Bartholomew beheld the Son of God on the chariot of the Cherubim. All the heavenly hosts were about him. He blessed the body of Mary.

She went and gave the message to the apostles, and Peter blessed her, and they rejoiced.

Jesus and the redeemed souls ascended into Heaven, and the Father crowned him. The glory of this scene Bartholomew could not describe. It is here that he enjoins his son

Thaddaeus not to let this book fall into the hands of the impure (quoted above).

Then follows a series of hymns sung in heaven, eight in all, which accompany the reception of Adam and the other holy souls into glory. Adam was eighty cubits high and Eve fifty. They were brought to the Father by Michael. Bartholomew had never seen anything to compare with the beauty and Glory of Adam, save that of Jesus. Adam was forgiven, and all the angels and saints rejoiced and saluted him, and departed each to their place.

Adam was set at the gate of life to greet all the righteous as they enter, and Eve was set over all the women who had done the will of God, to greet them as they come into the city of Christ.

As for me, Bartholomew, I remained many days without food or drink, nourished by the glory of the vision.

The apostles thanked and blessed Bartholomew for what he had told them: he should be called the apostle of the mysteries of God. But he protested: I am the least of you all, a humble workman. Will not the people of the city say when they see me, 'Is not this Bartholomew the man of Italy, the gardener the dealer in vegetables? Is not this the man that dwelleth in the garden of Hierocrates the governor of our city? How has he attained this greatness?

'The next words introduce a new section.

At the time when Jesus took us up into the Mount of Olives he spoke to us in an unknown tongue, which he revealed to us, saying: Anetharath (or Atharath Thaurath). The heavens were opened and we all went up into the seventh heaven (so the London MS.: in the Paris copy only Jesus went up, and the apostles gazed after him). He prayed the Father to bless us.

The Father, with the Son and the Holy Ghost, laid His hand on the head of Peter (and made him archbishop of the wholeworld: Paris B). All that is bound or loosed by him on earth shall be so in heaven; none who is not ordained by him shall be accepted. Each of the apostles was separately blessed (there are omissions of single names in one or other of the three texts). Andrew, James, John, Philip (the cross will precede him wherever he goes), Thomas, Bartholomew (he will be the depositary of the mysteries of the Son), Matthew (his shadow will heal the sick) James son of Alphaeus, Simon Zelotes, Judas of James, Thaddeus, Matthias who was rich and left all to follow Jesus).

And now, my brethren the apostles, forgive me: I, Bartholomew, am not a man to be honoured.

The apostles kissed and blessed him. And then, with Mary, they offered the Eucharist.

The Father sent the Son down into Galilee to console the apostles and Mary: and he came and blessed them and showed them his wounds, and committed them to the care of Peter, and gave them their commission to preach. They kissed his side and sealed themselves with the blood that flowed thence. He went up to heaven.

Thomas was not with them, for he had departed to his city, hearing that his son Siophanes (Theophanes?) was dead: it was the seventh day since the death when he arrived. He went to the tomb and raised him in the name of Jesus.

Siophanes told him of the taking of his soul by Michael: how it sprang from his body and lighted on the hand of Michael, who wrapped it in a fine linen cloth: how he crossed the river of fire and it seemed to him as water, and was washed thrice in the Acherusian lake: how in heaven he saw the twelve splendid thrones of the apostles, and was not permitted to sit on his father's throne.

Thomas and he went into the city to the consternation of all who saw them. He, Siophanes, addressed the people and told his story: and Thomas baptized 12,000 of them, founded a church, and made Siophanes its bishop.

Then Thomas mounted on a cloud and it took him to the Molmtof Olives and to the apostles, who told him of the visit of Jesus: and he would not believe. Bartholomew admonished him. Then Jesus appeared, and made Thomas touch his wounds: and departed into heaven.

This is the second time that he showed himself to his disciples after that he had risen from the dead.

GOSPEL (QUESTIONS) OF ST. BARTHOLOMEW

This is the Book of the Resurrection of Jesus the Christ, our Lord, in joy and gladness. In peace. Amen.

Peter said to the apostles: Let us offer the offering before we separate. They prepared the bread, the cup, and incense.

Peter stood by the sacrifice and the others round the Table. They waited (break in the text: Budge and others suppose an appearance of Christ, but I do not think this is correct: 4 1/2 lines are gone then there are broken words):

table . . . their hearts rejoiced . . . worshipped the Son of God. He took his seat . . . his Father (probably, who sitteth at the right hand of the Father). His Body was on the Table about which they were assembled; and they divided it. They saw the blood of Jesus pouring out as living blood down into the cup. Peter said: God hath loved us more than all, in letting us see these great honours: and our Lord Jesus Christ hath allowed us to behold and hath revealed to us the glory of his body and his divine blood. They partook of the body and blood—and then they separated and preached the word. (What is clearly indicated is a change in the elements: there is not room for a description of an appearance of Jesus: he says no word, and his departure is not mentioned.)

This writing may be better described as a rhapsody than a narrative. It bristles with contradictions of itself: Joseph and Philogenes both bury Jesus— Thomas raises the dead and will not believe in Christ's resurrection: and so forth. That Mary the mother of Jesus is identified with Mary Magdalene is typical of the disregard of history, and we have seen it in other Coptic documents. The interest of the authors centred in the hymns, blessings, salutations, and prayers, which in this analysis have been wholly omitted, but which occupy a large part of the original text. The glorification of St. Bartholomew is another purpose of the writer: the special blessings given to him recall the attitude which he takes in the Gospel (i. 1, 8) as inquiring into the mysteries of heaven, and seeing things which are hidden from others. Both Gospel and Book are specially interested in the Descent into Hell, the Resurrection, and the redemption of Adam.

Bartholomew (Nathanael) was told (in St. John's Gospel) that he would see the angels ascending and descending upon the Son of Man. This promise is fulfilled in the Gospel (i. 6, 231 and very often in the Book: in St. John we also read of his being 'under the fig–tree', and this was probably enough to suggest to the Coptic author of the Book that

24

he was a gardener.

A date is hard to suggest. The British Museum MS. is assigned to the twelfth century; the Paris fragments are older. That of the Coptic literature of this class is usually supposed to belong to the fifth and sixth centuries; and I think this, or at latest the seventh century, may be the period when the book was produced.

CPSIA information can be obtained
at www.ICGtesting.com
Printed in the USA
LVHW06s1824260318
571183LV00021B/1048/P